But you have such a pretty face

Crystal Senter-Brown

Gabby Girl Media

For exclusive content or to join the author's mailing list, visit www.butyouhavesuchaprettyface.com or www.crystalsenterbrown.com

For Mama.

Table of Contents

When I think of home

Ella's tambourine

so we decided
to sort through your belongings:
the church dresses, hats

stockings, thick- heeled shoes
worn not only on Sundays.
the nurse's aides had

thrown everything
into boxes even your
Bible, the one my

grandmother gave you
last Christmas. The three of us
stood by your bed, already

prepared for the
next patient, as my brother
searched each box for

your tambourine.
I know it has to be here
I said, remembering how
much you loved to
play it, how it would breathe
life into any "dry"(your word for boring)

church service. As I
felt the burn of yet another
round of tears welling up in

my eyes, I heard the
familiar jingle, as my
daddy pulled it out of

the last box. We left
everything else behind, told the
nurses to remove

your name from it all-
someone else could use it now.
On the ride home, no

one spoke, I held your
tambourine in my hands, my
fingertips tracing each

disc, it's hard, round belly
worn by a lifetime of use...

I could feel your hands, too.

For the lion fountain at Fred Miller park

the lion's roaring, metal mouth
swallowed our heads one by one, we stood
on tip toes, taking turns as the water
spewed out onto the fronts
of our shirts

we were too young to care about
staying dry and clean,
grass stained knees were
just fine with me
it was the summer of 1983,
and 100,000 degrees
so this lion fountain
was like gold, like an ocean flowing onto
our desert
after spending the entire day
skipping through rocky creeks, playing
hop scotch and doubledutch
touch football, swinging
twirling, dancing, eating peanut butter and jelly

the lion didn't have a chance of escaping us
so we took turns
feeding from his mouth
savoring this moment

everything would change by this time next year

everything always does.

George's departure (An Alphabet Poem)

For Granddaddy

As I was learning how to write my name in cursive, you were dying
Bound by tubes and breathing machines, you never once
Cursed the nurses or
Doctors, your faith allowed you to welcome the
End, even if we didn't. At
First I didn't believe you were actually
Gone, even when nannie took me by the arm
Heaving me up and over your casket
I didn't want to look at you, I
Just wanted to go home, rewind the clock back to seven days ago when you
Kissed me on my forehead and gave me cheetos before we
Left for school. But now, family
Members,
Not knowing what else to do, carried in cakes and fried chicken,
Orange jello molds and gallons of sweet tea, which we
Pretended to actually need. These strange people were
Quick on their feet, tidying the church fellowship hall, leaving neat stacks of
Red cloth napkins, ironed and ready for your wake. I
Sat in the front pew and watched you, your skin flat and ceramic-
Tinted by an amateur mortician, your suit jacket crammed
Underneath you, my grandfather was certainly no longer there. I still miss your
Voice, and the

Way you could find music and beauty in anything, from nannie's silver spoons to the toy
Xylophone, to the
Yellow
Zinnias in our garden, which have refused to bloom since the day you left.....

Home

When I am home, I am seven again
I am dusty pigtails and five best friends
I am hopscotch on hot sidewalks
wearing pink jelly shoes
I am 4th in line at the West Elementary pool

when I am home, I am the Christmas parade on Main Street
I am two tiny bare feet in Panther Creek
I am a Dairy Queen chocolate-dipped ice cream cone
and Saturday morning cartoons with my big brother Jerome

when I am home,

I am a tent revival on Wednesday nights,

I am brass offering plates with the crushed velvet lining
I am *Amazing Grace* and the taste of fried chicken
I am red kool-aid and switches picked for lickin's

When I am home, I am slowed down, *whole*
I am the daughter of Janice and Joe
I am Miss Frances' granddaughter
and Ella's twin,

I am the poet who remembers to stop just to take it all in,

when I am home.

Ladybug

1.
She wants to see and learn everything,
practice what magic can make the world spin,
she gives in too easily
and has never properly learned to hold a grudge

2.
She knows what red clay between her toes feels like
has cleaned chitlins fresh from the pig
and of course she has done her time in more than a few
Tazewell, Newport and Rutledge, Tennessee
Baptist tent revivals.

3.
She answers to
Ladybug
Babe
Pop
Mommy
Miss crystal
Babygirl
Chris
Booshane
Dotcom
Csb

Toute la femme
Chrissy

4.
She has never been to Venice, but longs to spend
two weeks canal-side
in the midst of poetry and sleep
white wine and chocolate ice cream

5.
She is Corey's bride and longtime lover
Adonte's nagging, *very uncool* mother
Janice and Joseph's only daughter
And Jerome's fuzzy-headed baby sister

6.
She misses Lynn, Melanie and Sasha
Ella, George and Eugene
she needs to call her daddy more
but is sure to write her grandmother by hand
every single week

7.

She speaks to strangers
forces frowning faces to smile
and she still has miles and miles to go
and she still has miles and miles to go

8.
She is at her best when in the company of children

surrounded by fingerpaints and chicken mcnuggets
board books and spongebob squarepants
identifying with toddlers and awkward teens

9.
She is often mistaken for naive
already mother by the age of 18
she erases normalcy and proceeds
to write her own destiny

10.
She finds a story in every face
a poem in every situation
sipping haikus for breakfast
nibbling on tankas for a midnight snack

11.
And these days, she is restless
wound up and ever-ready
a boundless ball of poetic energy
always dreaming a brand new dream

12.
She is a sweet tea- drinking
quick-thinking
peach cobbler- baking
country-girl
born and raised in the hills of upper east Tennessee
she is me
she is me

and
she
is
free!

Teen me

She's a believer in magic and shooting stars
orange Hubba Bubba and bumper cars

light as a feather, stiff as a board player
Mortal Kombat- fighter and Pac-Man ghost slayer

Prince poster-hanger and grassy hill tumbler
dollar pool-swimmer and good luck summoner

city bus transfer'er and baby balancer
sweet tea mixer and Kid-n-Play dancer

howling laugher and landline phone gossiper
cupcake baker and open mic rocker

toddler chaser and bedtime story reader
boo-boo mender and stray animal feeder

older now, but still a Tennessee girl at heart
lucky to have had Morristown as my start

excited to see what the next decade has in store
I am running through each and every God-opened door

thankful for the blessings god has given his girl
ready for this room, this city, this state,
the world!

That time when my brother Jerome was Evel Kneivel

First born,
brave and bold
curly haired, masked and caped
his apple red Converse give him a running start

He has been convinced by friends
that jumping five parked cars
wouldn't actually be *that hard*

and of course they all line up
chanting and cheering
Go go Jerome go! They howl

and soon,
he is airborne,
cape flying/
bike wheels spinning in mid-air

he soars up
up
    up
      up

and he feels the warmth of the sun

the freedom of flight
he feels the wind

the sky

and then

the crack
of pavement.

Welcome Home

(for Aunt Ann)

With barely enough
room for your own things you offered
me space in your home

saying *stay here for*
as long as you need to...
your sons carried

my luggage as I
balanced my baby boy on
one hip. You never asked

what happened, instead

you cooked dinner, bathed my son
and tucked us in for

the night. And for the
first time in many years, I could
breathe and collect what

was left of my sanity.
This became my first real
lesson in what it

means to be family,
what it means to have a home
to go to when the

world seems to be crashing
down around you. Sometimes all

you need is a warm

bed, a good night's rest
and someone who loves you enough
to hold you up

until you can fly
again
on your own...

Love

And ooooo, baby!

(a Jazz poem)

And ooo
I get
So lonely
When he
Ain't here
My body
Prefers
His, my
Lips were
Made to
Kiss (him)
My arms
Just
Don't feel
Right if
He ain't
Between
'em, my

Body
Prefers
His, my
Hands won't
Grab on
Nothin'
Else but
Him even
If I
Tried, man
They'd probably
Just raise
Up and
Say *woman*
are you
crazy?
Gimme
Some' a
That sweet
Brown, sugar
Only
He can

Give, he
Simmers and
Bubbles
Up from
My soul
Reminds
Me of
Why I
Have lips
And hips
And when
He ain't
Next
To me?
Ooooo baby,
I don't
Even
Wanna
Breathe. My
Thick legs
Prefer to
Be around

Him, when
He ain’t
Near ‘em
They just
Downright
Protest!
They sit
All crossed-like
Won't do
Nothin!
And I
Guess to
You this
Sounds kinda
Crazy but
My baby
Breathes air
Into my
Lungs, he
Adds an
Extra
Spring to

My knees
I even
Have this
Special
Melody
Only
He can
Make me
Sing
I say
Ooooo weeee!
Baby
You were
Made for
Me! And
He just
Smiles with
His arms
Around
Me.
Just
Like it's

‘sposed to be.

Backsliders

Sunday mornings are
our only chance to dance under
the covers, your slick

skin against mine, the
scent of our dreams dancing in
the air. You touch me

there, where prose is born-
where my heart beats- we speak the
same language no

one else knows. We stay
in bed past noon, you become
my lunch, my belly

full of you. Your kiss,
still on my lips, I dream of
more Sundays just like this...

Before dawn

the sound of your breath
on the outskirts of a dream
flies high above me/

thick with hours of
night, rest and love, in the dark
your lips find mine. The

hour is before
dawn, before the first stretch/ first
yawn of good morning/

the warmth of you wraps
around me, my soul sings your
glory/ you light the

night with love/ peeling
away the grit of the day/
our renewal/

a web, carefully spun,
each and every morning
like this one, we still

don't need words/just legs
around waist, breasts against back
we beg the sun for

a few moments more/
our love is simple and
divine, you are my

air/ my breath/ my soul
my everything/ you are the
reason my heart sings.

Driving lessons

I need you
to slide down
into the depths
with me

peel away
the 'has been'
to reveal
the 'will be'

align your mouth
with my smile
make no mistake
that you are the reason for my waking
each and every day...

let me map out
your every inch
as you teach me
the subtle bend of your road

so I can drive you all night long
even with my eyes closed.

First bath

For Aunt Carolyn

When the baby came
my stomach was opened,
stripped, gaping sardine can
peeled back to reveal my
ten- pound boy, held high
mouth round & screaming
my prize.

The days that followed
were met with whispers
no celebratory cigars
or birth announcements
I returned to the one- bedroom home the three of us shared.

You didn't even come right away;
You had school, your mama had to work
your sister and brother had church and
I spent seven days learning to bathe him

barely even able to bathe myself.

My aunt, somehow knowing
arrived at our home with basin in hand
filled it with ivory soap and hot water
and bathed me, as I had bathed him

We slept in mama's bed that night
three generations
warm
clean, new.

Flirt

Your shoes are shined
like brand new dimes
hair shimmering with coconut oil

your skin is satin
black like the night
your teeth, little seashells, sweet and pure

you're so smooth that the ocean follows you all around
and your mamba makes the world dance and
I don't know your name
but I know your stop
and the sound of your gum pop-popping in my left ear.

I just wish I could make time stand still
just long enough to feel the warmth your skin
next to me you are like a chocolate cloud
and I wanna scoop you up and *suck you in*

But you don't know me from anybody else
we all ride the same train
you've never spoken my name
but in my mind?
we are already married with kids
white picket fence
stock dividends
bushes neatly trimmed
a nanny named Kim
and so deep in love

Perhaps one day I'll get the courage to say
join me
after work for coffee
(or whatever follows meetings like that)
and your hat pulled snugly
maybe you'll approach me and agree to join me

and we'll sit and sip
and chat about this and that
and fall in love
and run away

maybe one day

But for now?
I'll watch you from my seat
awaiting the day we will finally meet
and tumble into this life in my mind
In due time, baby,
you'll be mine.

Loving out loud

He hates opera.
says hip hop is the future!
I nod - say nothing.

Turn it down!! I beg.
he's happy when his music
harasses the birds.

While driving, we're more
like strangers than man and wife,
one- third of our lives

have been spent this way:
in his car, fighting about
which station to play.

As the steam rises
from my ears, he calls me "dear",
turning the channel to

NPR, where we
listen to other people
fight about nothing.

He knows my strange ways-
he has helped write my story.
Seeing me at my

very best, and worst,

he wipes my tears, calming me
with just a glance.

He is my Sunday
revival, my sonnet, when
I can't find the words-

he taps his fingers
along my spine, pulling the
poems out of me.

He sails my spirit
to the clouds…who needs music
when love's this loud?

Lucky jeans

I secretly envy
your favorite blue jeans
every stitch
button
crease
and seam
because although they mean
nothing to you,
they spend every daylight hour
doing everything you do
sure, every night they are tossed on the floor
piled up, and abandoned
by your bedroom door
but oh, how I long
to spend just one day
as a crease at your thighs

or a button at your waist…

Re:Ignition

In anticipation of year fifteen,
meet me/ between blinks
right when you think
you have figured me out

before you even start to dream out loud
spin my thoughts on the clouds
in your sky

treat my eyes to the silhouette of you
undressed before the sun comes up
before the normal morning routine
when it's just the two of us

find my spirit sliding

seeking yours/ between our sheets

make room for our new souls

who have yet to meet...

This is why I love you (For Corey)

I fell in love last night,
it's been awhile

I like the feeling of getting up heart heavy,
mind filled with thoughts of you
and me
and life
and time spent with you alone

I fell asleep last night
your kisses still on my nose

the air still invaded with the words we shared as we planned our future

and house

and babies

And maybe it won't come out that way
maybe you won't stay right here

but all I know is that I love this feeling
this heart-heavy feeling
this baby don't ever leave me feeling
this *only you can give me* feeling

this feeling of happiness
of comfort
and strength

and this
is why
I love you.

Twenty-first morning

In time I am sure
I will re-learn the sounds of
our quiet home. You

have not slept here for
weeks, I cannot conjure up
the courage to call.

It was my fault you
said, that last evening when
we sat on the floor

in our living room.
I assumed you to be the
naive one, didn't

think you had in fact
seen it all. Knew everything-
the calls, what was said-

and instead of the
expected outburst of screams
broken dishes, torn

clothing, knives tearing
holes in our rented sofa
you quietly wept,

for hours. This side
of you was new to me as
the tears fell, dotting

your pressed shirt and tie.
Your eyes welled, pleaded with
why? Never again

I promised, next time
I said- I'd think of you first
I'd think of us first

I knew I was cursed
even as a teenager/
wide hipped- wild girl- bred

from a long line of
other wide hipped-wild girls- who
never thought about

how those long nights hurt
the ones who loved them most. I
tried to ignore the

burn that settled in
my core-at age twenty one
I really tried to

stay faithful. But it's
too late. You are gone. I will

find a new love like

you, who I will take
under my gentle wings and
sing my sweet song of

deception. But right
now, my soul yearns for the slow
subtle way you would

kiss me good morning.
I cannot sing just yet. Not
until I can forget

how you picked up your
suitcase from the floor, slamming
the door behind you.

Where they have books and things

I caught you watching
me, between the bookshelves, your
eyes peeped through wire

rimmed glasses, small brown
marbles with lights flickering.
Did you see me before

I saw you? Or did
my soul spread out to find yours
behind the double

doors? This space was made
for learning and reading, for
exploring new things

for building strong brains-
not for this. I lower my
eyes, a half- attempt

at diversion, but
it's no use, your eyes, your thoughts
have made their way in-

spinning into the
world that transforms "just classmates"
into something more

I slip out the side
door, the burn of your stare combs
through my hair onto

my neck, traveling
down my spine into my skirt
tickling my bare

thighs, teasing between
my knees and onto my calves
to the tops of my

feet and out through my
toes. Nothing has ever singed
my spirit like this

one gaze, I take one
step out into the light of
this New England day

unscathed and relieved
that I escaped you for now-

at least until next week…

The Weight is Over

Beautiful me

oh, how I love my hips

that dip and swivel

more than a double serving

baby-bearing, wide as all outside kind of hips

they are beautiful, graspable hips

and oh how I love my lips

that part and sing

that kiss and smack

the kind all lipsticks pucker up and pray for

they are beautiful, kissable lips

and oh how I love my hands

that can whip up a meal

and then write a business plan

they can soothe a crying baby, they're strong enough to move the earth!

they are beautiful, capable hands

and oh, how I love my legs

that twist and turn

that twirl and spin

dance and bend

they are beautiful, strong and solid legs

and oh how I love my brain

a brain that is eager

a brain that craves more

an a plus earning, scholarship deserving, dean's list kind of brain

it is a beautiful, knowledge-absorbing brain

and yes,

I love every part of me

the over-sized parts,

the too-small parts

and all the parts between

I love the parts that dimple

and the parts that sag

even my stretch marks

ain't that bad!

And to think it took over thirty years

for me to finally be able to see

that the most important,

compliment deserving person

will always be

me,

beautiful me!

Chunk

Lane Bryant jeans
bustin' at the seams
I breeze past your lingering stares
there are many ways to say fat in our language
but I, sir
do *not* fit that profile
from my super-sized thighs
to my triple scooped boot/teasing your glances
dancing alone by mirrored walls
cause you know
they say that *nobody*
wants to dance with a fat girl
when in fact
everybody wants to dance with a fat girl

somehow they love that chunk
that funk
that our thinner sisters never quite got
now I'm not saying
we're better than they are
we just
have a little more to offer
we smother you in our sweetness
we smell like pound cake with cherries
we move like smoothies down your throat
I've got pounds of juice where most have ounces
And I will pounce when beckoned
you better come correct or don't come
you'd think you'd know by now how I will take you
break all of your misconceptions of the bigness
baby you can't mess with this!

I make you afraid of how you feel
making you sleep outside my window singing love songs
in early moanin'
for me
pleading for me
seeing me from across the room
pants a bit too tight
I cause fights in rooms of peace
women stare in disbelief
when I walk out with the same man they came in with
this chunk cannot be messed with

you need your daily dose of funk
your vitamins a,b, and chunk
you see yourself falling into addiction
can't sleep without our fattening friction

soon night will come
and you'll put away those
toys that boys think they need

those silly girls
resembling matchsticks
with weave tickling the
backs of their knobby knees
and you'll see us the free
hair short as can be
squeezing into a size 18
and then you'll realize that maybe you are a
fiend
for the bigness
for the
chunk.

The droopy boob haiku

When, after visiting my grandmother for a week in upper east Tennessee, a duct taped letter containing a crisp $100 bill arrived in the mail. A note attached simply read:

"buy a new bra. Be
sure to find one that lifts and
separates. Good luck."

-love, Nannie

The uninvited guest

At the very least
you allow me a moment
of peace during the

early morning, in
the shadows of my room you
watch me, but do not

speak. Not until I start
my day do you begin to
make your way into

my space. At first you
are just a subtle nudge, but soon
you take up every

room in my home. As I
hurry to make coffee, you
are next to me, then

on top of me, so
heavy I can hardly breathe.
As I am brushing

my hair you are there
with each unbearable stroke.
You are the one thing

I would rather not

count on- predictable like
the air I breathe

like the steadiness
of my heartbeat, you are with
me, always. At night

when you have tired
of me, you retreat into
your corner, at least

you allow me to
sleep. But I know 8 hours
will pass and soon you

will return, the burn
of you swelling up from my
floorboards.

For my Sisters

A ballad for the shade-throwers

You probably never learned how to shine

with your mama baggin' groceries at the five and dime

and your daddy busy chasin' short skirts up the block

you stayed in your tiny bedroom, watchin' the clock

Waitin' for your turn

your day

your time

when you could finally be at center stage, all up in the spotlight

But you spent so much time down in the ditch

that the only thing you've mastered

is how to be a B……..ad, bad, woman

So when you met me,

of course you wanted to throw shade

hate swirling all around you,

so deep you had to wade through

your eyes all squinted thinking I wanted to be you

When in reality I was content with just being me

And I love all of me:

the sunny me, the bright me, the educated me, the happy me

the round me, the country me, the sassy me, the nappy me

the sleepy me, the hungry me, the fed up me and the praying me

the onlybusfareinmypocket me and the car note-free me

And then you realize that you can have what I possess

even on your handmedown dress days

and your D's on test days

as long as you have your *keep getting up* days

you'll be happy, healthy and have no need to throw shade

So get up off of your *whoa is me* chair

slide some gloss on your lips, run a comb through your hair

take hold of this moment that is your life

claim your future as a mama, a daughter and a wife

God gave you everything you need to succeed

he even gave you friends like her, him and me

friends who are even willing to take the lead

and once you realize your blessings, you'll be free

And the grocery-baggin' mama and skirt chasing daddy

the years of thinking only a man can make you happy

will all be things you can bury in the past

and you'll find the one true love that will last and last

And you'll sing, you'll dance, you'll twirl, you'll shine

won't even need to want for what is mine

because you'll have all you'll ever need, and more

So now that you know, what are you waiting for?

A poem for black girls

(a tribute to Nikki Giovanni's "Poem for black boys")

You carry fire with you everywhere you go ,
hands on hips, head titled to the side
big brown eyes full of wonder,

no one can be like you!

You will never have to pay for
full lips, wide hips, curly hair
you already have it naturally, because can't you see?

No one can be like you!

Your skin shades- from sunlight to Bermuda brown
no sunbathing is needed, you wake up beautiful
naturally tanned,

no one can be like you!

And your beautiful mane? Oh, it can do anything!
From afro puffs to micro braids, stocking cap weaves to finger rolls
short cuts, ponytails, flat iron straight-

no one can be like you!

And your lips? Plump, and glistening
no injections needed here
and you have what others pay hundreds for-

no one can be like you!

And your hips? Wiiiiiiiiiiiiiiiide as all outside
squeezing into your favorite pair of jeans
size 0, 2, 8, 10, 12, 14 (16, 18, 20,24) and proud of it-no one can be like you!

You watch as others stand in line
saving to buy what you already have
stand talk black girl this world is yours!

No one can be like you!

Affirmation

I have finally hitched my dreams to the moon
after taking up all the available space in *that* room
that was filled with hungry crabs biting and clawing at my feet,
I am now ready for any challenge I have yet to meet

I have climbed out of that desolate tomb
shed myself of everything I thought, or assumed
I am now breathing, laughing, dancing, singing and free
in search of *everything* God has for me

And now that I have cast my cares to the wind
I am finally able to begin again
using my past fears as stepping stones
making success, peace and happiness my home

So as long as I am breathing, I will climb

In search for everything that is rightfully mine

no longer frozen in fear by the test

I am confident, beautiful, focused and blessed!

Can you stand the "reign"?

1

although she is barely 19
she has mastered the art of the twerk and pop,
the prettiest girl in a sea of filth
she is a living, breathing, lollipop.

2.

9 months pregnant with baby #5
living in the projects on the lower east side
no future plans dance inside her head
except "what kind of purse should I buy?"

3.
corporate executive, a wall of college degrees
determined and successful, she is on her way,
corner office swaying high in the sky
squeezing 48 hours into a 24 hour day.

4
sweet 17, rockin' Baby Phat jeans
bubble gum lip gloss, Nikes on her feet
bound for college next year, future as bright as the sun
but she has yet to meet her self-esteem

5

almost 83, born and raised in Mississippi
happily residing in her three room shack

she's lived through it all, a living testimony
remembering when she was once hated just because she was black

6

she stands, arms raised, ready to worship
bible in her hands, cross around her neck,
she has chosen God as her life-long companion
visiting Him on Sundays and every chance she gets

7.

thirty four, single and loving it
entering year four of her five-year plan
she's showing the world she can have it all
even without a man

seven different stories, seven different journeys
yet all tied with one common thread
we can be easily spotted out of the crowd
by the crowns we wear upon our heads

and while some of our crowns sparkle and shine
with gems of diamond and pearls
others wear crowns that are missing their jewels
broken and shattered by the weight of the world

they may have once reigned and ruled the world
but now they are down-trodden
and instead of their fellow queens lifting them up
they are often pushed aside and forgotten

but their fairytale does not have to end this way
not if we decide today to make a pact
to go out into the world and find our forgotten queens
determined to them back

and some of them won't return easily, know this for sure
some of them will fight you out of fear,
but she'll slowly start to come around
once she sees the jewels in her crown begin to reappear

and once she is re-crowned, watch out!
She'll be up and on her way!
And the only thank you that you will need

is the smile upon her face

so what are you waiting for? Get out the door!
There is no better day than today!
Because who knows, the tables may turn
and she'll have to save *you* someday.

Last call

By the time the words
last call
wail across the crowded dance hall
he has already staked his claim on you

assuming,
after all the things you allowed him to do
under the swirls of the blue disco ball

that the only reasonable next step
is to find your own bass-line
back at his place

so when he tilts his face toward yours
and whispers,
gently
join me
you immediately begin to think about
your *his and her* shower heads

and empty bed

that always seems so cold at 4 a.m.

and he takes you by the hand,

to find your coat and keys

and says

maybe we can grab a bite to eat

says

I know a place we can get something sweet. Do you like waffles? Orange juice? Coffee?

and you nod, like any nice girl would do

making him think he actually has a chance with you

and he can already see his hands in your pants

his lips stamping the edges of your thighs

even though he has yet

to even look you straight in the eyes

he wants to make you feel like the prettiest girl on earth

or at least the prettiest girl in the city

or at least the prettiest girl on this side of the gritty,

rundown bar

and as you make your way to his car
you look up and check your surroundings
watching other girls, who look just like you
making their way into their own chariots of hell
sure to be dismissed before they've even watched the sunrise
from the window of a downtown hotel

you, suddenly
reach out to grab your car keys
and as you climb into the driver's seat
he begins the *please baby baby please*

because you know better than to dive in over your head
you're much too precious to end up in a rented bed
listening for all the things that will remain unsaid
counting the cracks on the unfamiliar wall
only to wait for days/ weeks/ months
for his *I promise to call*

for you are old enough to know
last call doesn't mean

last chance to be happy
or *last chance to find your knight in expensive shoes*

so you point him in the direction of another hungry, lonely girl
who probably also likes waffles
and orange juice
too.

Mean (black) girls

Head wraps
don't magically
make you deep

just like nose rings
don't make you
a queen

you can
let your hair
knot up
and twirl down
your back

you can
raise your clenched fist,
proclaiming your blackness

but if every other word

is against
your sisters
who don't
mirror what you believe
and stand for?

then you, ma'am
are a phony,

writing poems
with $20 words
but when things fall down,
you're running with the herd

and if that ain't enough?
you knock your sisters for
rockin' a perm

claiming they're
rejecting their blackness,

showing yet another level of your wackness

and this may
seem like an
angry poem,

but it's been
a long time coming

I've been humming
the lyrics to it
for far too long

this is a song for you
begging you
to be true to yourself

peel back the mask
you show the world

I bet you didn't know
you could be supportive and kind
and still be a (real) black girl.

Monsters in the closet

You were the one my mother warned me about
every night, in my bedtime stories
you were the monster
hiding in my closet , never appearing
until mama had left the room

you quietly assumed the position of gentleman
the absolutely perfect man
even pleasing my grandmother with your southern hospitality
but who knew
that beneath all that charm
was a well-dressed rattlesnake, fully intent on doing me harm

even your hands were serpents
grasping for any opening/ you were
hoping for a princess and you got me
the real me, earring in my nose, braided up ponytails and fishnet pantyhose

but oh baby, if you could see me now!
This lovely, proud girl with her chest puffed out
the one who, years ago, would have never worn this skirt with these legs
who stopped following her heart, and started using her head

so you are free now
to climb back into your closet get lost

among old coats and mismatched shoes, perhaps
a new girl with a case of the blues,
who really wants to know what primal fear is all about
will come your way, open your door,
and let
you
out.

My first love

I have always wanted you
even before I was supposed to

Back when I was supposed to be brushing Barbie doll heads
and playing hopscotch,
I craved papercuts, gasping audiences
squealing microphones and
Langston Hughes

I remember the way you'd sway my day into a song
made me long for you

even when you didn't make sense or rhyme

I wanted to give all my time

to you

even when history papers were due,
I wrote you
I *breathed* you

now life is crowded, overworked,
tasks stacked like dominos on my desk,

almost making me forget how much I dig you

my skin pale from lack of stage lights,

I am yearning
for the hustle of the highway

I catch you watching me
when I am silent,
you're waiting for me to pick up my pen
and begin again

you send pieces of yourself to me

via blog posts and anthologies
napkins and borrowed books

you're always looking for me

I won't abandon you for much longer,

I can't
my breath is shallow

brain overworked by everything serious
everything mandatory

everything dull

I am missing the poems

that used to sing across my room
sweeping like a broom

clearing the dust from my heart.

I'll start tonight
even if the words crumble

and land on the floor
that's alright

they say "it's kind of like riding a bike"
familiar like trikes with training wheels
and no, it don't pay the bills

(and it probably never will)

but it chases the blues away with one swoop of pencil on pad
oh baby, you are the best I've ever had,
please don't ever leave me
promise you'll always have a song for me

even when I have forgotten my own words

remind me of the fire I set each time I step to the mic…

don't let me forget
don't let me forget.

Revival Time

The church is full
a sea of purple
and pastel greens
among the sea of club-sharp and Easter-pristine

God sits, proudly

and although next week may show a
different scene,

since some were dragged here by their nannie
or *Big Mama*
Aunt Mary or cousin Jean

this week, there's a person in *every* seat
God is working His way through the crowded room

And Pastor Steve knows just what to do

modifying his word to welcome them all in

eyes once lowered are suddenly all on him
could he be talkin to me? Someone says
How could he know 'bout that? another says

and the old school member with the giant hat,
holds hands with the first time visitor wearing torn blue jeans,
baby phat
nightclub stamp still on her right hand

everyone is welcomed
hugged
kissed
and shown just what it means
to be loved, unconditionally, by a Christian

no matter where you came from
even if you don't have a church hat...

Endangered Species

(Poems for Men and Boys)

Brother

Notice how your mere presence scares them
watch how they scatter when you enter the room

see how they can't even look at you
without their heads lowered, voices hushed and muted?

They know all about your history,
how your veins flow freely with the blood of kings and queens

some men try to duplicate what you have, but they never could
it doesn't even come in all sizes, cannot be bought in a store

it's the way you move-even through the doorway,
your confidence entering the room before you do

and I don't expect to understand
how it feels to be a black man, I know your eyes have seen more
than I have in my lifetime

even though your skin shines coconut brown like mine
even though your hair ropes and twists like mine

it seems as though you arrived here long before your time
a staggering stature, the pure definition of swagger

you are the kind of man all women look for
the one we'd all choose to spend every waking moment with

you will always be the one, over all others we will choose
when we close our eyes at night- we even dream about you

a history of tragedy, upsets and nonsense
has left you guarded, always on the defense

you may be misunderstood, but your heart pumps strength
strength that stretches beyond the norm

so the next time you don't believe the strength you have
and how much power you exude?

Notice how your mere presence scares them
watch how they scatter when you enter the room.

Dandelion

I sometimes wonder
if you can sense the way
your energy fills

a room, the way knees
begin to buckle and bend
at the mere sight of

you? How sharing the
same space often ignites the
smoky, firework

filled- frenzies. You are
buttoned up/ combustible/
a windsor/ (k)not for the

weary/ even on
your off-day, heat seems to seep
from every

ounce of you. And when
your smile begins to descend
upon your lips I

quietly picture
my own, brushing against them.
The assembly line

of adoration
forms and soon there is no room
for me/ they dive in

hips first, swimming in
your contagious grin. But you
quickly bore of this

side-show you know you
will never be without a
warm bed/ you know that

there will always be
the hungry ones, the eager
ones, struggling

up from the cracks of
the earth like dandelions
after the first rain in May.

Disposable daddy

She said
television daddies always come home
and that even after ten hour days,
they never say "later"
when asked to play

pouring invisible tea with a smile
successfully scaring monsters away
every single night

on TV they are always present,
a towering oak,
stable and rooted,
protecting everything and everyone they love

they are hard workers, successful
teaching life skills, paying light bills
and ballet school tuition

my Daddy is like Barbie's baby's Daddy
she says
pointing to the box on the floor
with the painted-onto-the-background-Daddy

he is disposable, replaceable,
an unnecessary prop

easily thrown away with the box

but still she waits for him to come back
some day
his absence is evident in her every move

for now, she keeps her TV tuned
to *Leave it to Beaver*
And *the Cosby Show.*

For AJ at seventeen

and when the boughs broke
and you made your entrance into my world
your stuttered choke cried out for me
a living, breathing siren

your blue eyes
opened right away
2 weeks late, already lazy
my own mama inspected you, counting fingers and toes

at age 19 I hadn't quite figured out
what mother's should do
the right way to be a mommy
how to best raise you

but raise you I did, and we grew together
learning the world- not always kind but
you were mine, and I
always imagined you preferring to be by my side

and this is why
today hurts me more it would otherwise
when conversation with you is always
chopped up, awkward, strained

you prefer the *tap-tap-tap* on keyboards
cell phones, and video games

acknowledging me only during meal times
you don't even have time to say "mommy" as I am simply "mom" now

and in my fits of anger, when I don't understand if this is all part of becoming a man
the angels who have traveled this path before me, fly down, their hands on my shoulders
assuring me that it does in fact *get better*

and as soon as I feel like I cannot go another moment in the midst of this
spinning in a whirlwind of hormones the little boy in you appears to me
sometimes abruptly, your eyes will soften
your words, calmly asking- *would you like me to wash the dishes* mommy?

and suddenly I forget about the grumpy days,
the shrugged shoulders,
the many ways you have learned to push every
available button I possess

and in between your bursts of sunlight I am happy to serve as personal taxi
allowance distributor

fetcher of forgotten lunch money and homework assignments,
washer of gym shorts and school uniforms
for I know this moment will never come again

you are a growing, learning
growling teen, and I will be here for you, *whatever that may mean*

and years from now I am sure we will laugh
over coffee or even a glass of wine

I value this time, even the bumps and bruises
even when you test my patience, yet again
I hope that when we come out of this we
will not only be mother and son,

but also
friends.

For Daddies

You may not know it now
but *this* day

filled with all things
little girl

all things glitter and shine
ruffled socks and tap shoes
little girl squeaks and squeals

is shaping her
into the woman she
will ultimately be

when you are there
every time she reaches out for you
when your hand
touches hers
when you walk

through parks, skip across sidewalks
she is learning
what it means to be
valued
and loved
and honored
and safe

and when you touch her face with
your hands, she learns
what it means to be loved by a man

but if you are absent
if you are unreachable, if her walks
through the parks are solo
with
no one to hold her hand she will
reach out for anything
anyone who looks like they may care

when in reality
they'll only want her in pieces

she'll be broken apart into
selfies and computer screen shots
with the true essence of her being
erased

and the side she'll shows to the world
will be distorted, wild,
showy, bare
she will
speak like she was never schooled
as she looks for you
in every passing face

so this day
when you see her smiling face again
touch her
kiss her
read to her
love her
hold her close to you,
promise her
that you ain't goin nowhere

and *mean it.*

The luckiest girl on earth

he stops to tie the
strings of her pink reebok's with
light-up heels/ as she

notices me, she squeals
I am this many holding
up one thumb two

fingers. They come here
every Friday for
ice cream, something

he has always done
with each of his three daughters
as soon as they learn

to walk. Trying to
focus on her shoes she talks
and talks, pointing to

the sky, then the tree
she says *see that bird? He knows*
me! Her father, the

ever-serious
one, all buttoned up, tied
and pristine, begins

to smile widely. He
knows her sunshine is too bright
to dim and she is

good for him. As they
walk away, she begins to
skip, heels lit and

flickering. Her braids
swinging, walking with daddy,
she is the luckiest girl on earth.

Played

She spends most of her day
happily encased
sailing along strange highways

not minding at all
just awaiting nightfall,
when he is ready to play

she stands at attention
her smooth, shined silhouette
hot brass, awaiting his sweet melody

only his fingers and mouth
can change her tune from a hum to
room shaking, vibrating shriek

she is the only lover
he has ever wanted, his wife
the woman of his dreams

after seeing the way
his lips touch hers,
all the faces in the room turn from hues of brown to envious green...

she is perfectly made

just what he needs
we watch, as he plays her brassy physique

so we wait our turn
arms folded, cheeks burning
jealous of a metal we will never be.

Poem for black men

My closest friend asked me once
Crystal why do you only write sad poems?
And I told him:
I write about black men loving black women
needing black women
leaving black women

I made him think of the world in a whole different way
made him think of a new phrase
think of a different way to say how I feel
maybe I c*ould* write about trees and fields
but that wouldn't be "keepin' it real"

I could try not to think about the violence

black men shot down, beat down
strung out on crack
and for every black man we lose
we lose a whole generation of beautiful black people

black lawyers
black judges
black floor sweepers
and cooks

we should uplift our black men as kings
and teach them how to sing

show them how to dance instead of shoot
write poems instead of selling drugs
fight for equal rights instead of fighting each other in the streets

take time to meet them
climb deep inside them
tell them you love them
make them love you
make changes in your life and in their lives too

remember all of our men that are filling the ground
make a difference by *being* the difference
and maybe once this is done I won't write sad poems anymore.

The boogeyman

His million-dollar grin and gentleness
makes everyone want to welcome him in
pulling back chairs and opening doors
he leaves his hat on to hide his horns

and since he does not wear the mask of a monster,
or a ghoul
he easily makes his way over to you
sliding into your sacred space with ease

lacing up to skate between
your hopes and dreams

and to the outside world, he is a saint
painting the image of never-do-wrong

when in reality he preys on girls just like you
who end up doing things they swore they'd never, ever do

and when you meet him you won't know he's the boogeyman, at
first
for you are cursed with the trusting, double wide heart
wanting him long before he even notices you

he does not hide in closets

or under bunkbeds
he slips behind ponytails,
afros and dreads

he is the shimmer in your lipgloss,
the jewels on your ears
he's everything your mother ever feared,

so when you meet him
and trust me, you will
do yourself a favor and step to the side
ignore the warmth cascading down your thighs
shake off the tummy filled with butterflies

and run fast, girl

run!

The death of you

I still mourn the last
time your lips touched mine, write out
sympathy cards when

it becomes too hard
to even say your name/ when
the mere thought of you

causes my knees to bend
and buckle, stomach burning
and I cannot breathe.

You said that this was
just a test, a chance for you
to try something new

but you never knew
that *I chose you.* I sought
you out. And those long

nights you'd awaken
at 3 a.m. were because
of me. We shared the

same view of the moon

but from different rooms, the light
flickering on our

bedroom walls. And now
that your calls have stopped, and my
life resumes it's slow

methodical pace,
I can still taste you, in the
air that surrounds me

my heart, heavy with
the space you left behind, still
beats, still struggles to

keep me breathing, at
least until I remember
how to, on my own

again..

When everything was new

His fitted hat is tilted
to one side, his large hands shoved into
his jean pockets, baggy
and current, yet ironed
perfectly, with a smile as wide
as all outside.

he doesn't even see
me at first, as his nose is
pressed and flattened against the glass
of the nursery
a sea of screaming, bundled
hours-old babies, housed in
identical plastic bassinets.

even in a sea of fifty,
he knows which one has
been placed under his
wing, which one he will sing
lullabies to, softly and off-key.

to me, they all look
the same, but before she even

had a name, he
loved her. Her piercing
cry makes his heart pound,
butterflies tumbling around in his stomach,
nervous that he won't know how
to be a father, since
he never knew his own
until he was already grown

but now, a sense of purpose
beams from him like sunshine
felt by him for the very first time
he leans over to me,
and says,
(with his teary eyes
still wet and reddened)

that one is mine.

About the Author

Crystal Senter-Brown was born and raised in Morristown, Tennessee to a bass-playing Baptist preacher (Joseph T. Senter) and a visual artist (Janice Treece-Senter), Crystal was introduced to poetry at the age of six.

Crystal is the recipient of several awards including the 2013 Black Leadership Award, the 2012 Bay Path college Pathfinder Award and the Harold Grinspoon Award for her children's book *Gabby Saturday*. She has also been featured in Essence Magazine, Vibe Magazine and Redbook Magazine.

She is the author of *Doubledutch, Gabby Saturday* and *The Rhythm in Blue* which is currently being made into a feature film. Her stage credits include The Vagina Monologues and The Wiz. Her poetry has appeared in *The Thick Chronicles, His Rib, Wordplay II, Point of View, The Women's Times* and *The Republican*. Crystal has been a Justice of the Peace since 2001 and officiated hundreds of weddings in Massachusetts.

When she's not writing, performing or saving the world, she lives in New England with her husband Corey, and son Adonte.

Find Crystal online at www.crystalsenterbrown.com

Other Books by Crystal Senter-Brown

Gabby Saturday

It's Saturday, do you know what that means? It means Gabby gets to wear her yellow dress and put away her jeans! Gabby's Mama is taking her on an adventure!! The Gabby Saturday series promotes self-esteem and literacy among African-American children, specifically young girls.

www.gabbysaturday.com

Doubledutch

Doubledutch is the first collection of Crystal Senter Brown, and all poems included in this book were written between 1996 and 2006. Some poems are biographical, others are simply observances. Doubledutch skips through topics everyone can relate to: Love, parenting, relationships, poverty, employment, solitude, dieting, size acceptance, cheating hearts and everything in between.

Sample chapter from

The Rhythm in Blue

Chapter One

Mason Joseph was fed up.

His fiancée was turning into a wedding-crazed maniac, his career was going nowhere and his days seemed to be one endless loop of nothingness. He knew he was destined to do more, but how could he focus in the midst of sheer chaos? He needed a few days away from his life. His wedding was in three weeks and he was afraid if he didn't allow himself some time to regroup, he may not be making that trip down the aisle after all.

But how would he get a break? And where would he go? He didn't want to go to a hotel. He couldn't go to his mama's because he'd be too busy answering questions about why he was there to actually get any rest. In his heart he knew there was only one place he could go: to Jasmine's.

Jasmine had certainly offered her home as a resting place before. She lived just outside of Norfolk in Blue, Virginia, and far away from the hustle and bustle of the city. A part of him wondered if it would be a wise decision to spend a few days with her, given the fact that he was an almost-married man. But almost and married were two different words. Besides, he hadn't seen Jasmine since her latest breakup, and he knew they had lots of catching up to do. As soon as he dialed her number he began to feel his stomach knot up. The phone rang twice and just before he was going to hang up, he heard Jasmine's voice on the other end.

"Hey, Mase!" she said, recognizing his number from her caller ID.

"I'm coming," he said. Two words. Nothing more.

Mason stopped home to pack a duffel bag with enough clothes for a couple of days. He scribbled a note for his fiancée that simply said I'll be away for work until Monday. Luckily, his fiancée was so engrossed in planning the wedding, she would actually welcome this break from him.

But Mason felt selfish running away, Real men were supposed to stick around through the storm, right? Mason wanted Sasha to stop stressing over the wedding but the more he insisted, the more she stressed. Sasha wanted Mason to take an active role in every decision to be made about their wedding, from the location to the color of the pew flowers. But Mason didn't care about any of that, he just wanted to show up and get married. Going away for a few days was the only thing he could think to do.

The drive to Jasmine's house was always a peaceful one, thanks to the smooth familiarity of Virginia's highways. Mason knew the roads from his college days. He knew the cleanest rest stops and even some of the people working in the roadside diners.

An hour away from Jasmine's house, he started getting excited. A warmth always came over him any time he was going to see her. He chalked it up to friendship and nothing more, but to be honest, he never had the same feeling with any of his other friends. Jasmine was different. She made him remember who he used to be, before he became a lawyer, and long before he became Sasha's fiancé.

When Mason pulled into Jasmine's driveway and noticed the familiar flickering of candles through her living room windows, he immediately felt at ease. Her house was set back from the street, and it always reminded Mason of the gingerbread houses he used to read about when he was a child. He threw his tattered duffel bag over his shoulder and knocked on her door.

"It's open," Jasmine called out from the kitchen.

As soon as Mason stepped inside he could smell what he missed the most these days: dinner cooking in the kitchen. Sasha was far from domestic, and most of their meals came from the local take-out restaurants. Sasha tried to cook one time during their entire relationship, and that attempt ended with the fire department being called to the scene. But what Sasha lacked in the kitchen she more than made up for in other ways. She had a great personality and everyone seemed to love her.

Jasmine peeked her head around the kitchen door and waved her hand to say hello, with her phone balancing between her ear and her shoulder. She was wearing the apron he had bought her as a gag Christmas gift last year. The apron read "Full-bodied, sweet and thick. And the wine ain't bad either."

Mason kicked his sneakers off under the coffee table and leaned back onto her sofa. Jasmine's home was the only place he felt relaxed enough to truly sleep. He picked up the remote to change the channel to the game but noticed Jasmine had already done that for him. She was not a sports fan, but she always watched it with him when he visited. He locked his hands behind his head and propped his crossed legs up onto the ottoman. Within a few minutes Jasmine reappeared with a plate of food, and as she put it down in front of him he marveled at the plate and then at her.

He devoured his dinner in what seemed like seconds and before he could even ask, she was already bringing him a second plate. He reached out to find his once empty glass refilled and even a pair of slippers sat next to his feet. She was a powerhouse in this city, but when they were alone in her home she was submissive, willing to do whatever it took to make him happy.

Jasmine finally rejoined him with her own plate of food, sitting cross-legged next to him on the sofa. She had taken the apron off and Mason laughed at her alligator head slippers.

"Where'd you get those slippers?" Mason asked.
"Oh, you got jokes, man? I slaved over a hot stove for you and you got jokes now?"
She pretended to try to snatch his dinner plate from him. He laughed.
"I'm just kidding"
"So, how you been, friend?" she asked, taking a bite of her food.
"Tired," he said. "Just tired."
"You're always tired," she said, laughing. "Is that why you came here?" she asked.
"That. Among other things." He joked as he leaned closer to her.
"Now you know we are NOT going there, man. Not even a little bit!" she said, firmly.
"I'm not even talking about that! I just needed a break. Sasha is driving me crazy! Every single day she is asking me to pick a color for the flowers and a color for the linens. Who cares about that?"
"SHE does." Jasmine snapped. "And you should too! Mason, I swear you can be so self-centered at times!"
"ME? Sasha is THE QUEEN of being self-centered."
"So why are you marrying her?" Jasmine asked.
Mason lowered his head. "I love her," he said softly.

"I know you do," Jasmine said. "You just gotta learn how to take

the bad with the good. You knew she was a maniac when you proposed to her. Why would she change now?" she asked.
"You're right. Hey, on another note, I was hoping you would read over my community center idea. I think I can get some funding for it if I can get it completed by the end of the month. The proposal is in my bag," he said, pointing to his leather messenger bag on the recliner.

"We can check it out later," Jasmine said. "Finish the game, I'm going to my kickboxing class and when I get back, we'll…chat. Try to stay awake, okay? I know my cooking be puttin' brotha's DOWN!"

He watched her walk away. Her hair was piled on top of her head, and she was wearing one of his t-shirts, one he had probably left at her house years ago. She was beautiful. She looked back and caught him watching her.
"What are you lookin' at, man?" she said, with one hand on her hip and her head tilted to the side.
Mason smiled. He was just happy to be there.
Mason dozed off and the next thing he knew, it was midnight. He got up to see where she was, and he found Jasmine sitting in her office with his proposal. She looked up at him.
"This is amazing, Mase," she said.
"You think so?" he asked.
"Yes!" she said "You definitely could get funding for this!"
"Do you really think it could work?" he asked her, squeezing onto the futon next to her, even though there were two additional seats in the room.
"I don't see why not. We don't have anything like that in our neighborhood. And you added a sports component too? I love it! I

think it's ready to go as it is! No one has ever thought to create a community center like this!" Jasmine said.

Mason's heart swelled with joy. He asked his fiancée Sasha to look over his project idea a million times before and each time she would wave him away for some sort of wedding planning activity. He had been carrying around the folder for months now, and all it took was for Jasmine to know how important it was to him. She didn't think twice about spending her evening reading his plans. Her selfless love for him is why Mason had always cared so much about her.

As Jasmine continued to read, Mason leaned his head back onto the futon and looked around. Jasmine's office was more like a sanctuary. The walls were painted a shade of blue that reminded him of the water he swam in when he visited Bermuda the year before. She had citrus and sage candles burning, which gave the room a warm and inviting feeling. Mason's eyes traveled the length of the room and he read each degree and award that hung on Jasmine's wall. He also looked at the dozens of framed photos of friends, family, and people Jasmine had met over the years. But there was one photo of a person he didn't recognize.

In the picture, Jasmine was smiling bigger than Mason had ever seen before, and there was an unknown man with his arms wrapped around her waist. From the background of the photo, Mason could tell they were either on a cruise ship or on an island. Wherever they were, Jasmine looked happy.
"Who is this?" Mason asked her as he held up the photo. There was a little jealousy in his voice.

"Why you all up in MY business, Mr. I'mgettinmarried?" she said.

She knew immediately that she had touched a nerve with Mason when he fell silent, focusing his attention on the mystery man's massive hands.

"Hey, man, I don't wanna make you all stressed out, I know you have enough of that at home, but have you even talked about some of the things YOU'D like to see at your own wedding? I mean, is it all about her?"

Jasmine decided not to go any further with the conversation because it was none of her business. She didn't even HAVE a fiancé so who was she to make demands on him? She handed his folder back to him.

"Thank you for letting me read your proposal, Mason. You've always been so motivated!" she said, motioning for him to follow her to the living room.

They settled onto the couch and Jasmine slid into Mason' arms with an ease of familiarity. Mason's long arms wrapped around Jasmine as she leaned her head against his chest. Mason missed the feeling of Jasmine against him. They had a comfort level with each other that surpassed friendship.

Around 2 a.m., Jasmine stood up and stretched, reaching toward the ceiling on her tiptoes.

"I think I'm gonna call it a night. I made up the guest room for you and set the coffee pot to brew at six. You can use the guest shower if you want. What do you want for breakfast?"

"I don't eat breakfast," he said.

"You do now," Jasmine said "well, at least you will while you're here. Sleep tight, okay?" she said.

When Mason stepped into Jaz's guestroom he felt like he had

stepped into his own private oasis. The king-sized bed was already turned back, sandalwood candles flickered on the nightstand. Mason couldn't wait to take a shower. He just wanted to wash away the worries of his day. After his shower, he settled into bed and pulled the comforter up to his chin. He was almost asleep when there was a knock at his door.

"Mase?" Jasmine called out through the door. "Can I come in for a minute?"

"Yeah," he said. "Come in!"

Jasmine's came in and sat down on the bed next to him. He could smell the coconut oil she always used after she showered.

"I'm worried about you," she started.

"Why are you worried about me? I'm okay! " he said, immediately on the defense.

"I just feel like you're unhappy. I mean, I've never seen you like this before. And maybe you're just tired. I don't know. I shouldn't have even come in here, it's so late!" she said, laughing.

"Did you enjoy your shower?" she asked, lying back on the pillow. Her arm grazed his as she settled in to the other side of the bed.

"Yes! I could have stayed in there all night!

"I'm glad, I just want you to get some rest while you're here," Jaz said. "You always stay so busy! You're always on your grind!"

"I try," he said, "but if I'm so much on my grind then why can't I get a break? I mean every single part of my life is a mess. Everything. My relationship. My job. The only sanity I have is when I come here or when I actually make it to church on Sunday morning."

Jasmine looked at him, her lips curled.

"Mason don't even try to lie and say you go to church. Because you know as well as I do that you ain't seen the inside of a church in

months."
Mason couldn't argue; she was right.
"All I know is, I need a break. I need something to happen, and soon," he said.

Their faces were inches apart.

"I need something to happen soon, too," she said.

Mason wondered if they were still talking about their lives in general or this very moment. He couldn't help but to imagine how it would be if they could spend the night together.
Jasmine leaned in, resolving any doubts he had about just what she meant, as soon as her lips touched his, his phone buzzed on the nightstand, bringing them both back to reality.
Sasha appeared on the caller ID. It was Mason's fiancée.

Mason and Jasmine froze, lip to lip.

"Well, that's my cue," Jasmine said, getting up. "See you in the morning, homey," she said before clicking the door shut behind her.

"Yeah. See ya," he said to Jasmine.

End of Excerpt